About the Book

What lies ahead for the newly married couple on the cover of this book? Will they have children and live a happy, fulfilled life? Can there be such a thing as the truly happy family? Such a family may be the exception, but is God content with a Christian home where there are constant upsets and quarrels? Is there a good way to live, according to New Testament teaching?

This short book, written in 1894, is a surprisingly modern look at Christian family life for couples newly married or celebrating their Golden Wedding! JR Miller shows how Paul's teaching on the duties of husband and wife can produce harmony, although he says many have misunderstood this teaching and taken it to unbalanced, unscriptural extremes, causing tension or even an impossible relationship. It is clear that in a Christian family, not only the parents, but the child, or children, have a vital role to play in creating a happy home life.

JR Miller writes: "This book may come into the hands of some whose home happiness has been shattered. ... It would be a comfort to the author if these simple words should put fresh hope into a discouraged heart, and thus be the hand to help restore the home to its true place."

Secrets of Happy Home Life

JR Miller
(1840-1912)

First published in the United States of America 1894
This edition is taken from the 1894 British edition

This White Tree Publishing edition
©White Tree Publishing 2019

This paperback ISBN: 978-1-912529-25-4
Also available as an eBook ISBN: 978-1-912529-16-2

Published by
White Tree Publishing
Bristol
UNITED KINGDOM

More books on www.whitetreepublishing.com
Contact mailto:wtpbristol@gmail.com

Scripture quotations from The Authorized (King James) Version. Rights in the Authorized Version are vested in the Crown. Reproduced by permission of the Crown's patentee, Cambridge University Press.

WHITE
TREE
PUBLISHING

Chapters

About the Author

James Russell Miller was an amazingly prolific Christian author. In addition to having the post of Editorial Superintendent of the Presbyterian Board of Publication, he was the pastor of several Presbyterian churches in Pennsylvania and Illinois during his working life. He was born on March 20, 1840 near Frankfort Springs, Pennsylvania. His parents had a total of ten children, but his older sister died before he was born. When James was about fourteen years old, his father moved to a farm near Calcutta, Ohio. In the new home James was as popular among his schoolmates as he had been in his Pennsylvania home.

We can see when reading about James Miller's early family life, how it is that he was able to write this book with great understanding about family life in a positive way. His biographer, John T. Faris, (*The Life of Dr. J.R. Miller: Jesus and I Are Friends* 1912) tells us that "The young people of the neighbourhood delighted to gather at the Miller [James's parents] fireside to enjoy one of the evenings of good fellowship for which the household was noted. It is easy to understand this when the lovable James had lively sisters, one of whom he described in fascinating manner is a letter to a friend, written after he went out into the world:

"'Your letters always remind me of a little sister at home whose wicked pranks are never to be forgotten, and whose letters always come filled with little bits and wit and sarcasm. She delighted always in teasing me when I was at home, in continually playing tricks with my letters, hiding my books and papers, and otherwise endlessly annoying me – but always with such good humour, and with such a quiet, innocent air, that, no matter how evil disposed, I could not for the world get angry with her. However, she knows very well that her big brother is very good natured and never apt to grow angry, and, moreover, that he enjoys teasing quite as well as she does. She is a good girl, and next to my mother the dearest on earth to me.'"

Faris also tells us that family prayers in Miller's family home, when he was young, were given absolute priority over everything else. There was to be no reading of a single Bible verse and a brief prayer!

Miller married Louise King in 1870. They had three children. He died in the Philadelphia at the age of seventy-two in July 1912, having been used by God to bring a great blessing to many thousands through his various pastorates, and to countless readers through more than thirty Christian periodicals, and through the sale of more than two million books in his lifetime.

White Tree Publishing has plans to publish eBooks editions of some of Miller's full length books in 2019. Please see our website for updates.

Publisher's Introduction

This short book is a helpful look at the way Christian families are – or could be – run in accordance with God's will. Far from recommending the (non-scriptural) "Children should be seen and not heard" and "The woman must keep quiet and know her place" pronouncements often associated with Victorian families, Miller sees an important (and Scriptural) role that *every* family member needs to play in order to achieve the "Happy Home Life."

This paperback and the identical eBook are from the British printing of 1894, the same year as the first American edition. The American edition had the subtitle, "What Have You to Do With It?" which doesn't sound particularly helpful or friendly! This subtitle is omitted in the British printing. The reference in the author's Introduction to the Civil War, is of course to the American Civil War – 1861-1865. (England had its own Civil War from 1642-1651.)

Full details and cover illustrations of our other Christian books, non-fiction, fiction and books for younger readers are on our website:

www.whitetreepublishing.com

As always with our Christian non-fiction books, we have inserted references to Bible quotes in brackets [thus], where these are missing in the original. It may be that the original authors believed they were writing to readers who were so familiar with the Bible that references were unnecessary, but we believe it is important for all our readers — whether familiar with the Bible or not —to be able to check the verses and context in their own Bibles.

Original Introduction

One summer afternoon during our Civil War, some Southern generals were sitting under a tree, when suddenly a shell from a Northern battery crashed over their heads. The officers hastened to seek a safer place. But one of the party lingered; and the others, glancing around, saw him stooping to the ground as if he had found something of great value.

The crashing of the shell through the branches had torn a bird's nest from its place, and hurled it to the ground. And the general of armies was gathering up this nest, with its sacred burden of young birdlife, to replace it among the branches.

This book may come into the hands of some whose home happiness has been shattered – its torn fragments lying now on the ground. It would be a comfort to the author if these simple words should put fresh hope into a discouraged heart, and thus be the hand to help restore the home to its true place, amid the branches of the tree of love.

Chapter 1

The Home

HOME is among the holiest of words. A true home is one of the most sacred of places. It is a sanctuary into which men flee from the world's perils and alarms. It is a resting place whither at close of day the weary retire to gather new strength for the battle and toils of tomorrow. It is the place where love learns its lessons, where life is schooled into discipline and strength, where character is moulded.

Out of the homes of a community comes the life of the community, as a river from the thousand springs that gush out on the hillsides.

We are all concerned in the making of some place home – our own home. One instrument out of tune in an orchestra mars the music which breaks upon the ears of the listeners. One discordant life in a household mars the perfectness of the music of love in the family. We should make sure that our life is not the one that is out of tune. We do not need to worry about the other lives; if each looks to his own, that will do.

When our Lord sent His disciples out to preach, one of His instructions was, "Into whatsoever house ye enter, first say, Peace be to this house" [Luke 10:5]. Peace is a good word. It is more than a salutation. Falling from the Master's lips it is a divine benediction as well. Peace, too, is a fruit of grace which includes all that is sweetest and most divine in Christian culture.

It is especially suggestive of the harmony of love which is the perfection of beautiful living. Christ's peace is a blessing which comes out of struggle and discipline. Well, therefore, does the salutation "Peace!" befit a Christian home, which ought to be the abode of peace.

What are some of the secrets of happy homemaking? The answer might be given in one word – Christ. Christ at the marriage-altar; Christ on the bridal journey; Christ when the new home is set up; Christ when the baby is born; Christ when the baby dies; Christ in the pinching times; Christ in the days of plenty; Christ in the nursery, in the kitchen, in the parlour; Christ in the toil and in the rest; Christ along all the years; Christ when the wedded pair walk toward the sunset gates; Christ in the sad hour when farewells are spoken, and one goes on before and the other stays, bearing the unshared grief. Christ is the secret of happy home life.

But the lesson may be broken up.

Chapter 2

The Marriage

THE MAKING of a home begins before there is a home – it begins in the days when the life-choices are made. There are many unhappy marriages. There are families sheltered in houses which are not homes. A happy home does not come as a matter of course because there has been a marriage ceremony, with plighted vows and a ring, and the minister's "Whom God hath joined together, let no man put asunder," and a benediction. [Matthew 19:6 and Mark 10:9].

Happiness does not come through any mere forms or ceremonies. It has to be planned for, lived for, sacrificed for, prayed for, ofttimes suffered for.

There must be a wise choosing before marriage, or it may be impossible to make a happy home. At few points in life is divine guidance more sorely needed than when the question of marriage is decided. A mistake then will cast its shadows down all the years to the close of life. Many a career is blighted by a foolish marriage. Wedded happiness depends greatly on reverent, prayerful, deliberate, wise choosing before marriage.

But now the choices have been made – carefully made, we will say. The happy day has come. The plighted lovers stand at the marriage-altar. Taking the woman's hand, the man says to her, "I take thee to be my wedded wife, to have and to hold, from this day forward, for better for worse, for richer for poorer, in sickness and in health, to love and to cherish, till death us do part, according to God's holy ordinance; and thereto I plight thee my troth."

Taking the hand of the man, the woman says to him, with slight verbal variations, the same words. The two are pronounced husband and wife, and go forth to begin their wedded life together, no more twain, but now one.

The happy pair are in their own home. It may be a fine, great house, with rich furniture, costly pictures, and all the elegances of wealth; or it may be a little house with four rooms, cheap furniture, homemade carpets, and bare of adornment.

It makes very little difference what the size of the house, or what its furniture may be. The happiness of the home does not depend on the house or on what it contains. The people who live in the house make the happiness – or mar it.

The husband has his part. He must be a good man. Not every man who marries thinks of the responsibility he assumes when he takes a young girl away from the shelter of father-love and mother-love, the softest, warmest nest in the world, and leads her into a new home where henceforth his love is to be her only shelter. Well may the woman say as she goes to the marriage altar,

"Before I trust my fate to thee,
Or place my hand in thine;
Before I let thy future give
Colour and form to mine;
Before I peril all to thee,
Question thy soul tonight for me.

Does there within thy dimmest dreams
A possible future shine
Wherein thy life could henceforth breathe
Untouched, unshared by mine?
If so, at any pain or cost,
Oh, tell me before all is lost."

Adelaide Anne Procter

Chapter 3

The Husband

No man is fit to be a husband who is not a good man. He need not be great, nor rich, nor brilliant, nor clever, but he must be *good*, or he is not worthy to take a gentle, trusting woman's tender life into his keeping. Of course he must love his wife. Without love there is no real marriage, and ceremony and ring and vows and prayer are only empty formalities.

He must love his wife and be always her lover. The world has read and heard quite enough moralizing about a wife's duty to be always winning and attractive, retaining the charm of girlhood amid all cares, toils, and sorrows. Of course; but is a husband under less obligation to love his wife and always to be lover-like? This is a good rule, which should work both ways.

But affectionateness, however desirable, is not all that is needed in a husband who would do his full share in happy home-making. Life is not all sentiment. We cannot live on ambrosia. Happiness must have a very practical basis.

A good husband must be a good man – manly, true, worthy, brave, generous, a man whom a noble woman can respect and honour all the days of her life. He must be a sober man. No man who comes home under the influence of intoxicating drink, even occasionally only, is going to do quite his share in making happiness for the woman who has trusted her all to him.

He must be a man of pure, unblemished life, whose character is above suspicion, whose name will always be an honour and a pride in his own home. The husband has a great deal to do with the question of home happiness.

Chapter 4

The Wife

The wife, too, has a responsibility. The prosaic arts of housekeeping are far more important factors of home happiness than many people without experience imagine. Ruskin talks to young women of the etymology of the name wife: "What do you think the beautiful word 'wife' comes from?" he asks. "It means 'weaver.' You must either be housewives or house-moths, remember that. In the deep sense, you must weave men's fortunes, and embroider them, or feed upon them, and bring them to decay."

Home is the true wife's kingdom. There, first of all places, she must be strong and beautiful. She may touch life outside in many ways, if she can do it without slighting the duties that are hers within her own doors. But if any calls for her service must be declined, they should not be the duties of her home. These are hers, and no other one's.

Very largely does the wife hold in her hands, as a sacred trust, the happiness and the highest good of the hearts that nestle there. The best husband – the truest, the noblest, the gentlest, the richest-hearted – cannot make his home happy if his wife be not, in every reasonable sense, a helpmate to him.

In the last analysis, home happiness does depend on the wife. Her spirit gives the home its atmosphere. Her hands fashion its beauty. Her heart makes its love. And the end is so worthy, so noble, so divine, that no woman who has been called to be a wife, and has listened to the call, should consider any price too great to pay, to be the light, the joy, the blessing, the inspiration, of a home.

Men with fine gifts think it worthwhile to live to paint a few great pictures which will be looked at and admired for generations, or to write a few songs which will sing themselves into the ears and hearts of men. But the woman who makes a sweet, beautiful home, filling it with love and prayer and purity, is doing something better than anything else her hands could find to do beneath the skies.

Chapter 5

Becoming One

Some marriages are unhappy. How can husband and wife live happily in their wedded life? Wedded happiness is a lesson that must be learnt. No two lives brought into this close relation can blend into one without self-discipline.

Marriage is the beautiful unfolding of many years. We are not married on any day, but all along; for love...

"...Yet always opes
Fuller and fuller with each day and hour,
Heartening the soul with odour of fresh hopes
And longings high, and gushings of wide power;
Yet never is, or shall be, fully blown,
Save in the forethought of the Eternal One."

James Russel Lowell

Ofttimes it takes a long while for a wedded pair to learn the lesson of living happily together. They are discouraged because such love as theirs does not yield perfect happiness from the very first day. It always costs to learn the lesson. The marble must waste as the image grows. There must be the cutting away of much in both lives. There must be restraint, self-denial, self-effacement, while they are being trained to live one life rather than two. Love is always discipline.

"For life, with all it yields of joy and woe,
And hope and fear – believe the aged friend –
Is just our chance o' the prize of learning love,
How love might be, hath been indeed, and is."

Robert Browning

Saint Paul lays down the basis for happy wedded life in the words, "Wives, be in subjection to your husbands, as is fitting in the Lord. Husbands, love your wives, and be not bitter against them" [Colossians 3:18-19].

Perhaps these instructions are not always well understood. Sometimes one of the counsels, and sometimes the other, is unduly emphasized. Some men insist upon the first: "Wives, be in subjection to your husbands." They interpret the words somewhat harshly, as if a wife were to be only as a child to her husband, or even as a servant, whose duty is to minister to his wants, to please him, to run at his every call and command. This is in accordance with heathen notions of the marriage relation, but it is not after Christian teaching.

It is to be particularly noted that Saint Paul nowhere says, "Wives obey your husbands." In our King James Version the word "obedient" occurs in one place; but in the Revised Version the counsel is that wives should be "in subjection to" their husbands. Indeed, however, the spirit of love is always that of subjection, of yielding, of serving, in all life's relations.

In another place, where Saint Paul gives like instruction, his words are, "Wives be in subjection unto your own husbands, as unto the Lord. For the husband is the head of the wife, as Christ also is the head of the Church" [Ephesians 5:22-23].

No doubt the husband is the head of the household, but what a responsibility this teaching puts upon him! His wife is to be in subjection to him, "as unto the Lord." He is to be to her what Christ is to the Church.

Chapter 6

Sharing and Serving

If a man will insist on his wife fulfilling her part, he must also insist on honestly fulfilling his own part – all the sacred duties which are his as a husband. What, then, is the husband's share in this happy home making?   "Husbands, love your wives, even as Christ also loved the Church, and gave Himself up for it" [Ephesians 5:25].

A husband is to love his wife. Is love despotic? Does love put its object in a servant's place? No; love *serves*. It seeks not its own. It desires "not to be ministered unto, but to minister" [Matthew 20:28]. It does not demand attention, deference, service, subjection. *It seeks rather to serve, to give, to honour.*

The measure of the love required by the husband is to be well noted: "Even as Christ also loved the Church" [Ephesians 5:25]. This is a lofty standard. How did Christ show His love for

His Church? Think of His gentleness to His friends, His patience with them in all their faultiness, His thoughtfulness, His unwearying kindness. Never did a harsh word fall from His lips upon their ears. Never did He do aught to give them pain.

It was not easy for Him at all times to maintain such constancy and such composure and quietness of love toward them; for they were very faulty, and tried Him in a thousand ways. But His affection never wearied nor failed for an instant. Husbands are to love their wives even as Christ also loved the Church, and gave Himself up for it. He loved even to the cost of utmost self-sacrifice.

There are men, however, who would do this, whose love would sacrifice even life itself for a wife, but who fail in daily and hourly tenderness when there is no demand for great self-denial. Hence the other counsel must be remembered: "Love your wives, and be not bitter against them" [Colossians 3:19].

More wives might complain of the lack of love in the little tendernesses than in great acts and manifestations. A true woman's heart craves gentleness. It is hurt by bitter words, by coldness, by impatience, by harsh criticisms, by neglect, by the withholding of the expressions of affection. Love craves its daily bread of tenderness.

No husband should deny his wife the little things of affection, the amenities of love, along the busy, trying days, and then think to make amends by putting a flower in her cold hand when she lies in the coffin. Will not conscience then whisper love's reproach?

"You placed this flower in her hand, you say,
This pure, pale rose in her hand of clay?
Methinks, could she lift her sealed eyes,
They would meet your own with a grieved surprise.

When did you give her a flower before?
Ah, well, what matter, when all is o'er?
But I pray you think....
That love will starve, if it is not fed,
That true hearts pray for their daily bread."

Julia CR Dorr

Chapter 7

True Love

No true wife will ever quarrel with the divine law that makes the husband the head of the household, if she has a husband who loves her up to the measure of the divine requirements for husbands, "Even as Christ also loved the Church" [Ephesians 5:25].

Such love never demands obedience, never demands *anything*. It seeks not to be served, but to *serve*. True love in a wife also lives to serve. Love *always* serves, or it is not love at all. The greatest in Christ's kingdom are those who serve the most unselfishly.

Husband and wife vie with each other in loving and serving. They mutually bear each other's burdens. The husband is the head, but he never says so; never reminds his wife of it; never claims authority; defers to her in everything.

The wife recognises her husband as head, honours him, looks up to him with pride and confidence – all the more because he never *demands* subjection. Thus true love in husband and wife never has any trouble about rights or place. Side by side they stand, these two wedded lovers, each a part of the other, each incomplete, a mere fragment without the other, but strong in their happy union in love.

But there are other elements in the composition of the home. Among the blessings which make happiness are the children who come with their sweet life and their holy gladness. Children bring care, and demand toil and sacrifice, ofttimes cost pain and grief. Yet the blessing they bring to a true home, a thousand times repays the care and the cost.

Chapter 8

Parenthood

It is a sacred hour in a home when a baby is born and laid in the arms of a young father and mother. It is the final seal upon their wedded love. It is the closing benediction of the marriage ceremony. It draws fragments of heaven trailing after it to the home on earth. Few deeper, purer joys are ever experienced in this world than the joy of true parents on the birth of their first child.

Much of home's happiness along the years is made by the children. They are also great blessings to their parents. Ofttimes they teach more lessons than they are taught. We say we train our children; but they train us, too, if we think of them as we should – as immortal beings come from God to be prepared by us for their mission. Sings a reverent mother over her child's cradle,

"My child, I fear thee;
Thou'rt a spirit, soul!
How shall I walk before thee?
Keep my garments whole?
O Lord, give strength,
Give wisdom for the task,
To train this child for Thee."

Jesus said of little children that those who receive them in His name receive Him. May we not, then, surely say that children bring great possibility of blessing and happiness to a home? If we receive them as Christ's messengers, as sent to us in His name, and entertain them as we would entertain Him if He had come in place of them, we shall get from them deep and rich good and joy.

A true mother is one of the holiest secrets of home happiness. God sends many beautiful things to this world, many noble gifts; but no blessing is richer than that which He bestows in a mother who has learned love's lessons well, and has realised something of the meaning of her sacred calling. One mother writes,

"God thought to give the sweetest thing
In His almighty power
To earth; and deeply pondering
What it should be, one hour
In fondest joy and love of heart
Outweighing every other,
He moved the gates of heaven apart
And gave to earth a mother."

G. Newell Lovejoy

A father also should be a blessing to a home. The modern tendency to put upon the wife and mother all the responsibility for the making of the home and its happiness, is not sanctioned by Christian teaching. The divine commands for the building of the home and the training of the children are given primarily to the man, although meant for both husband and wife.

The husband cannot evade the responsibility. His position as the head of the family puts upon him the obligation. Besides, it is not manly that a man should want to put the whole burden on her whom he calls "the weaker vessel." If his wife is weak and if he is so strong, let him remember that it is the privilege and the duty of strength to bear the heavy part of life's burdens.

There are parts of the home duty which a

woman can do infinitely better than a man. Men's hands are clumsy, and often hurt gentle hearts, when it was meant that they should give healing and help. The man has the heavy care of providing for the household. There are tasks, too, for which woman's gentler hands are better fitted. But let no husband nurse the notion that he has no responsibility for the happiness of his home, beyond providing food and raiment and other comforts.

His strong life should be the secure shelter beneath which his wife and children may safely abide. His character should be a continual revealing of the love and truth and holiness of God. He should live so that, seeing him day after day, his family shall learn to know the beauty of Christ. He is the priest of his house, and as such should both speak to God for his family and speak to them for God. Through him blessings should come to his home every day.

Chapter 9

The Children

Brothers and sisters have their part in making the home happiness. Yet not always do they live together so as to make the music of the home one glad, sweet song. Sometimes there is a lack of congeniality in their dispositions. Then ofttimes there seems to be the feeling that home affections do not need the culture that other friendships require.

We cannot be brusque, curt, or rude with other people, and expect them to bear patiently with us in spite of our unmannerly behaviour. But we are sure of our family – so we let ourselves believe – that we do not need to be gentle and thoughtful towards them.

So it is that in too many homes brothers and sisters live together year after year under the same roof, mingling in the household life, yet never forming close friendships, soul never knitting to soul, strangers to each other's inner life. Thus many rich possibilities of close and holiest friendships are missed.

Another thing that too often mars the home life of brothers and sisters is a spirit of control and criticism. Faults are seen, and openly, and not in a gentle way pointed out and reproved. What one does the others are apt to do; and thus the habit grows, until little but sharp speech and unseemly wrangling is heard in the home where the conversation might have so much in it of sweetness and profit.

These are suggestions of ways in which, in too many homes, one of the secrets of happiness is lost. It is possible for brothers and sisters to live together in a home so as to add greatly to the happiness and the richness of the household life, and to be comforts and helps to each other.

It is said that the poet sisters, Alice and Phoebe Cary, had a secret of happy living together which it were well if all brothers and sisters could learn. [Alice, 1820-1871, and Phoebe, 1824-1871, were poets who grew up on Clovernook Farm near Cincinnati, Ohio.]

[In *A Memorial of Their Lives*, 1876, Mary Clemmer wrote]: "Whatever one felt or endured, because of it she would not inflict any suffering upon her sister! No, not even if that sister had inadvertently been the cause of it. If one sister was out of sorts, she went into her own room, shut her door, and 'had it out' by herself."

These are good rules to be adopted in other homes. If we are feeling uncomfortable from any cause, we have no right, according to the law of love, to diffuse our uncomfortableness through the household.

If we are in any unhappy mood, in which we cannot suppress the ill-humour, we have no right to vent it in the circle of our loved ones, and would far better go to our own room, or out into the fresh air, alone somewhere, and stay till we have gotten back our sweet spirit again, so that we can scatter roses, not thorns, among our loved ones.

The possibilities of happiness and blessing among brothers and sisters can be realised only by cultivating the love that seeketh not its own, that is not provoked, that beareth all things, endureth all things, and never faileth [1 Corinthians 13:4-8]. Love's first lesson is that of giving up one's own way, denying one's self, suffering in silence.

Where this lesson has been learned, or is being learned in a household of young people, each thinks of giving *to* the others, not of exacting *from* them. Each cultivates gentleness and kindness. The speech of the home grows quiet and tender, is never loud nor angry.

The Golden Rule is the law of each life. There is love, and love that reveals itself in a thousand little ways of courtesy and thoughtfulness – nameless things, but things that make up a home happiness on which heaven's angels look down with delight.

Chapter 10

Family Life

Not for very long can any family life go on unbroken. While we may, we should live together sweetly, patiently, loving and serving each other in all beautiful and Christly ways

The daily home life of the household carries in it many possibilities of happiness which are not always realized in families. Some suggestions may be made. One is that love must prevail in all the family life. Let parents keep the confidence and affection of their children as long as they live.

One of the ways to make sure of this is never to tire of the little marks and tokens of love which children naturally give. The time never comes when it is unmanly for a man to kiss his mother. In the ideal home every child has a goodnight kiss for the parents before parting.

Let the children do their part, too, in showing affection. There are homes, chill and cold, which could be warmed into love's richest glow in a little time, if all the household hearts were to grow affectionate.

Another suggestion is that all family strife and contention should cease. Why should parents discourage their children by continually nagging and finding fault with them? Why should children dishonour their parents by disobedience, by rude treatment not showing the qualities associated with a son or daughter, by want of respect, by refusing to yield to the order of the home?

Why should brothers fail in the duties of civility and courtesy to their sisters? Why should sisters show no loving interest in their brothers, and fail to overshadow them as with angel wings? Why should brothers wrangle and quarrel, separate their interests, and not stand together? Why should sisters have their miserable little disputes, their envies, jealousies, and piques? Let there be peace in all the home life.

Another suggestion is that we should not grow discouraged, even if our homes are not yet what we crave. There are some who feel that the battle is hopeless; that they can never grow into a beautiful life and character in their present circumstances. That is a mistake. It is possible to grow into all the beauty of peace wherever we may be placed.

A lily finds its home in a black bog, but blooms into perfect loveliness. Suppose that your home life is discouraging, even to the last degree; yet you may live sweetly in the midst of it, through the grace and help of God. And who knows but that your sweet life may become the power of God to change the home life into heavenliness? Perhaps God has put you as leaven there, to leaven the whole lump.

I have known a girl go out of a godless, worldly home to college, to find Christ and return home a beautiful, earnest Christian. Then I have seen that home transformed in a few years, by that daughter's quiet influence, into an ideal Christian home.

At least, though our home is not what we would like it to be, though it lack warmth and tenderness and congeniality, still, while it is our home, it is our duty to stay in it contentedly, and grow in it into beauty. We know that Jesus lived till thirty years of age in a humble peasant home, with but little culture and education, amid the privations of poverty and hard toil. Yet He was not discontented there.

He did not complain of the narrowness and the littleness. He did not chafe under the limitations and the burdens. There His life grew into that marvellous sweetness, that wondrous beauty, that richness and greatness, which we see in Him when, at thirty years of age, He went out to begin His ministry. Wherever we are planted we, too, can grow into strength, nobleness, and loveliness.

Patience is another lesson in learning to live happily together at home. The children of a family have not all the same tastes. It is very easy to fall into the habit of criticising each other. We know how nearly Martha spoiled her home happiness, and her sister's too, by criticism. [Luke 10:40.] Criticism never fosters affection; you never loved anyone better for criticising you.

Usually the best service we can do to a brother or sister is to live a sweet, patient, beautiful, Christly life ourselves, leaving to God the fashioning of their lives. If they are true Christians, He is teaching them and putting His own image on their souls. We might mar this divine work by our criticism.

Suppose you went into an artist's studio and saw a picture at which he had been working for months, yet unfinished. Would you, not being an artist, take up his brush and begin to put touches here and there on the canvas? Each life of husband or wife, child, brother or sister, in your home is a picture which God is painting, and which is yet unfinished. Beware that you mar not His work! So let us be patient with one another at home. We all have our faults; we all make mistakes; but we can help each other more by loving patience than by acrid criticism.

Chapter 11

Christian Faith

The Christian faith is the great master-secret of all happy home life. The spirit of Christ alone will enable us to live together in perfect peace and love. The presence of Christ in the home is a perpetual benediction. We cannot be selfish, we cannot wrangle and strive, we cannot be bitter and unkind, we cannot be irritable and unreasonable, when conscious of the presence of Christ. If only we can make Christ an abiding guest in our home, and if we can keep ourselves aware of His being with us, our household life cannot but grow wondrously sweet.

Into every home, at some time, sorrow comes. Then it is that the blessing of faith is specially revealed. We do not see the stars till the sun goes down. The comforts of Christian faith do not reveal themselves to us in their richest light and peace till the darkness of sorrow rests upon our home. But there is light in the darkness when Christ is the guest. Here, for example, is what one bereaved Christian mother could say to a mother of living children:

"Mother, I see you with your nursery light,
Leading your babies all in white
To their sweet rest;
Christ, the Good Shepherd, carries mine tonight;
And that is best.

I cannot help tears when I see them twine
Their fingers in yours, and their bright curls shine
On your warm breast;
But the Saviour's is purer than yours or mine;
He can love best.

You tremble each hour because your arms
Are weak; your heart is wrung with alarms,
And sore opprest;
My darlings are safe, out of reach of harms;
And that is best"

Helen Hunt Jackson

Indeed it is true that when Christ is in a home, even sorrow itself becomes one of the secrets of happiness. Our Lord's beatitude says,

"Blessed are they that mourn: for they shall be comforted" [Matthew 5:4]. Homes that have never known grief may be very happy in love, and very bright with sweet gladness; but after sorrow has been a guest within their doors, and has left its messages and blessings, there is a depth of quiet joy never experienced before. The family fellowship is sweeter after there has been a break in the circle.

The love is tenderer when tears have come into its gladness. A vacant chair is a new and sacred bond in the household life.

"The heart that suffers, most may sing;
All beauty seems of sorrow born;
This truth, half seen in life's young morn,
Stands full and clear at evening.
The gems of thought most highly prized
Are tears of sorrow crystallized.

All beauty has in sorrow birth;
Heartaches inspire the poet's themes,
And shape the painter's, sculptor's dreams;
Such is the destiny of earth.
His beams the heaven-taught genius throws
O'er all, and all with radiance glows."

But it is only when Christ is in the home that sorrow sweetens the life. There can be no rainbow without cloud and rain; but neither can there be a rainbow, even with cloud and rain, unless the sun is shining through the falling drops.

The rarest splendours of happiness can be known only when sorrow's clouds have overshadowed the home and the rain of tears is falling. But unless the light of divine love is pouring through the tears, there can be no splendour of peace and comfort – nothing but darkness and cloud.

Chapter 12

The Christian Home

Few things we can do in this world are so well worth doing as the making of a beautiful and happy home. He who does this, builds a sanctuary for God and opens a fountain of blessing for men. Far more than we know do the strength and beauty of our lives depend upon the home in which we dwell.

The person who goes forth in the morning from a happy, loving, prayerful home, into the world's strife, temptation, struggle, and duty, is strong – inspired for noble and victorious living. The children who are brought up in a true home go out trained and equipped for life's battles and tasks, carrying in their hearts a secret of strength which will make them brave and loyal to God, and will keep them pure in the world's sorest temptations.

We may all do loving service, therefore, by

helping to make one of the world's homes – the one in which *we* dwell – brighter and happier. No matter how plain it may be, nor how old-fashioned, if love be in it, if prayer connect it with heaven, if Christ's benediction be upon it, it will be a transfigured spot. Poverty is no cross if the home is full of bright cheer. Hardest toil is light, if love sings its songs amid the clatter.

"Dear Moss," said the thatch on an old ruin, "I am so worn, so patched, so ragged, really I am quite unsightly. I wish you would come and cheer me up a little. You will hide all my infirmities and defects; and through your loving sympathy no finger of contempt or dislike will be pointed at me."

"I come," said the moss; and it crept up and around, and in and out, till every flaw was hidden, and all was smooth and fair. Presently the sun shone out, and the old thatch looked bright and fair, a picture of rare beauty, in the golden rays.

"How beautiful the thatch looks!" cried one who saw it. "How beautiful the thatch looks!" said another. "Ah!" said the old thatch, rather let them say, 'How beautiful is the loving moss!' For it spends itself in covering up all my faults, keeping the knowledge of them all to herself, and by her own grace making my age and poverty wear the garb of youth and luxuriance."

(Anon, The Children's Hour 1868)

So it is that love covers the plainness and the ruggedness of the lowliest home. It hides its dreariness and its faults. It softens its roughness. It changes its pain into profit, and its loss into gain.

Let us live more for our homes. Let us love one another more. Let us cease to complain, criticise, and contradict each other. Let us be more patient with each other's faults. Let us not keep back the warm loving words that lie in our hearts, until it is too late for them to give comfort.

Soon separations will come. One of every wedded pair will stand by the other's coffin and grave. Then every bitter word spoken, and every neglect of love's duty, will be as a thorn in the heart.

Thomas Carlyle [who had a close but tempestuous marriage], when he passed the spot where he had last seen his wife alive, would bare his old head in wind or rain, his features wrung with bitter, unavailing sorrow. "Oh," he would say, "if I could see her but for five minutes, to assure her that I really cared for her throughout all that! But she never knew it – she never knew it!"

We must give account for our idle silences as well as for our idle words.

"Comfort one another,
With the hand-clasp close and tender,
With the sweetness love can render,
And looks of friendly eyes.
Do not wait with grace unspoken,
While life's daily bread is broken;
Gentle speech is oft like manna from the skies."

Margaret E Sangster

More Books

White Tree Publishing publishes mainstream evangelical Christian literature for people of all ages. Christian non-fiction, Christian fiction, and books for young readers. Many of our titles are only available as eBooks. We aim to make our eBooks available free for all eBook devices, but some distributors will only list our books free at their discretion, and may make a small charge for some titles — but they are still great value! All our books are fully typeset. No "photocopies" or bad OCR. So check for our name, **White Tree Publishing**, before purchasing or downloading!

In our reprints of older books, long sentences and paragraphs are broken into shorter lengths, and modern punctuation is used for easier reading. Many books are sensitively abridged, but in all our books no doctrine or teaching is changed. The full list of published and forthcoming books is on our website www.whitetreepublishing.com.
Please visit there regularly for updates.

We rely on our readers to tell their families, friends and churches about our books. Social media is a great way of doing this. Take a look at our range of fiction and non-fiction books and pass the word on. You can even contact your Christian TV or radio station to let them know about these books. Also, please write a positive review if you are able.

www.ingramcontent.com/pod-product-compliance
Lightning Source LLC
Chambersburg PA
CBHW060621030426
42337CB00018B/3135